A Really Basic Introduction to

English Contract Law

By Michael A Lambarth

Text copyright (c) 2020 Michael A Lambarth

All Rights Reserved

Table of Contents

Chapter 1 – Introduction
Chapter 2 – Making a contract
Chapter 3 – Adverts and other things
Chapter 4 – Unilateral contracts
Chapter 5 – Some practical things
Chapter 6 – Consideration
Chapter 7 – The end of an offer
Chapter 8 – The terms of a contract
Chapter 9 – Discharge of contractual liability
Chapter 10 – Frustration
Chapter 11 – Mistake
Chapter 12 – Breach of contract
Chapter 13 – Remedies
Chapter 14 – Misrepresentation
Chapter 15 – Exclusion clauses
List of Cases
List of Statutes

Chapter 1 – Introduction

Welcome to "A Really Basic Introduction to English Contract Law". Have you ever tried to find introductory books about complicated topics, only to be completely lost after a few pages? Usually, the author starts the book by explaining how basic the book will be, and then appears to forget this altogether on the very next page when he or she starts to use words which you do not understand. Having stated that no previous knowledge is required, they very quickly start to assume that you know the meaning of specific terms, or they say that it would be helpful to know a bit about some other subject before reading the book. The fact that you have purchased a book which was described as a basic introduction to the subject seems to evade them completely.

This book is exactly what it says it is; a really basic introduction to English Contract Law. No previous knowledge of law is needed. I will explain everything in full as we go along and will not try to impress you with my knowledge of complex terminology. This book will give you a good understanding of Contract Law and how it works. It will help you understand your own contractual position in certain matters. It will also help you if you are undertaking any course of study where knowledge of contract law is required, such as law, business, management, accounting or finance. Needless to say, an introductory book of this nature does have its limitations. After reading through it, you will not be able to give detailed legal advice to other people. Nor will you understand the subject in depth, or be able to talk to a professional adviser on their own terms. It is, after all, a really basic introduction to the topic.

So who am I to think that I can write such a book? Well, I am a qualified higher education law teacher and a qualified solicitor. Hopefully I therefore have the skills needed to convey this subject in a clear and concise manner. I have spent many hours explaining the principles in this book to students, colleagues and clients, so I am convinced you will be able to follow what I am saying.

I have tried to keep this book as short as possible, so that it is manageable, and so that you don't lose interest or feel intimidated after just a couple of chapters. The other thing I have done is to try to keep things real and practical. Law is a difficult enough subject to grasp, without trying to do so in the abstract. Each chapter deals with different aspects and builds upon the last chapter, introducing different ideas as we go. This means that your understanding is automatically consolidated as you read and that you should be able to read this book from start to finish and end up with a pretty good understanding of what is going on. You shouldn't have to keep flicking back to previous sections to remind yourself of what you read yesterday, or last week. I hope that you will end up with a confident, basic understanding of the subject.

The law is correct as at January 2020 and many of the principles are likely to remain relevant for quite some time but, due to the changing nature of law, that is outside of my control.

I hope you enjoy the book.

Chapter 2 – Making a contract

We'll start by looking at how to create or form a contract. When we think of a contract we probably think of a written document which two people sign to signify their agreement to the terms in that contract. For example, the contract you might sign when entering into a new mobile phone agreement. However, we enter into many contracts, most of us on a daily basis, without ever really thinking about it. When I buy a sandwich from a local shop I am actually entering into a legally binding contract with the business that operates the shop. When I travel on public transport I am entering into a legally binding contract with the transport operator. The list goes on and on. We can often identify that a contract might exist by the movement of money. Most contracts involve some kind of commercial activity and therefore the payment of money by one person to another. Someone who enters into a contract is referred to as a "contracting party". We therefore say that they are "party" to the contract.

In some ways it would make more sense to start by looking at what happens when a contract is breached. For example, when someone fails to do something they agreed in a contract to do. Most of us do not think about our contractual rights until things go wrong. For example, if the sandwich I bought is out of date and therefore inedible, or the train for which I bought a ticket is cancelled. However, it is difficult to fully understand the rights that arise when contracts are breached without first looking at how contracts are formed. So this is where we'll start.

Let's meet Aaron. He wants to buy a car. He has just finished at university and starts his first full time job in a couple of weeks' time. He is really looking forward to it, but the job is located on the edge of town and a car would certainly make his life easier. He has £2,000 in cash which his parents have lent him, and he wants something small and economical.

Walking home one day he sees a car parked on the driveway of a house with a "For Sale" sign in the windscreen. He walks over to the car and has a look round it. The car is a small, blue hatchback which is a few years old but looks to be in good condition. As he is checking it over the front door of the house opens and Beth comes outside and introduces herself to Aaron as the owner of the car. They have a chat about the car generally and Beth confirms that it is in good condition as far as she knows. It has a full service history and whilst the mileage is high, everything seems to be in working order. Aaron quickly decides that he would like the car.

Contract law is based on agreement. In order for Aaron and Beth to enter into a legally binding contract they need to reach an agreement. In order to determine that this is the case, there are traditionally five main elements to a contract which need to be present. These five elements are offer, acceptance, consideration, certainty and intention to create legal relations. Don't worry about this terminology, I will explain it regularly throughout this book and hopefully it will become second nature to you in due course. The first of these elements is an offer. Let's see if we can identify one in our scenario.

Aaron wanders around the car one more time and then asks Beth how much she was looking to sell it for. Beth replies that ideally she would like to get at least £2,200 for the car. Aaron nods at her and continues to think about the car.

Do we have an offer yet? I don't think so. Aaron has simply asked a question and Beth has replied to it. An offer is where one person sets out the terms on which they are willing to be bound in a contract. The idea of an offer is that the other person will then simply be able to accept it, without adding any new conditions or changing any of the terms of the offer. The closest we get here is in Beth's response. She states that ideally she wants at least £2,200 for the car. But she is not offering to sell at that price, just stating her position. What we have here is the start of a negotiation. We are still waiting for the first offer.

Aaron tells Beth that he was hoping to pay less than £2,200 due to the age and high mileage of the car. After some thought, she tells him that she would let him have it for £2,100 if that resulted in a sale today. Aaron considers what she has said and then offers her £1,800 in cash today for the car.

We appear to have our first offer. In fact we have two offers here. Firstly, Beth offers to sell the car for £2,100. Secondly, Aaron offers to buy it for £1,800. An offer takes effect when it is communicated to the person to whom the offer is made. The person to whom an offer is made is often referred to as the "offeree", which is not a common word in everyday language. Probably easier to remember is that the person who makes the offer is called the "offeror". Again, this is not a common word but perhaps more memorable. If you forget which way round these terms go, then think of an employer offering a job to an employee, or a lessor renting a flat to a lessee, or a donor making a gift to a donee, all of which follow the same pattern.

Taking our offers in the order in which they were received, Beth makes her offer to sell the car to Aaron for £2,100. The offer was clearly received by Aaron at exactly the same time as it was made by Beth (she spoke it out loud and he heard it). The offer contained all the terms which are needed to allow Aaron to accept the offer. The terms were that he would pay £2,100 today and take the car away. Aaron did not accept this offer, but he didn't specifically reject it either. Rather, he offered £1,800 for the car on the basis that he would give her the cash today. Again this has all the main terms included to allow Beth to accept the offer if she was minded to do so.

In fact what Aaron has done is to make a counter-offer. A counter-offer can sometimes look very much like an acceptance (the second element required in the formation of a contract). The important distinction is that a counter-offer does not accept the original offer, but seeks to change it or add something new. Beth offered to sell her car for £2,100. Aaron effectively refused this offer and made a new offer to buy the car for £1,800. A counter-offer is therefore classed in law as a rejection of the original offer and the making of a new, revised offer. Should Beth refuse the revised offer (of £1,800) then Aaron cannot go back and accept the original offer which ended when it was rejected. Of course, he could make a new offer to buy the car for £2,100 and there is presumably no reason why Beth would not accept that offer, but technically *he* would be making the offer at that point because her original offer to sell at £2,100 has been rejected by his counter-offer. Rejection brings the offer to an end.

As we go through this book I will be referring to legal cases. These are real life situations which ended up in a court of law before a judge (or a number of judges depending on the court). The law of contract consists mainly of a series of judicial decisions. The main method of making new laws in the English legal system is for Parliament to pass an act, called legislation. A piece of legislation is also referred to as a statute and is basically a numbered list of legal provisions. However, there are few statutes which relate to the law of contract. Instead, the law in this area has been developed by decisions of judges in courtrooms all over the country over the course of hundreds of years. Once a legal point has been decided by a senior court, it binds other courts so that when a judge comes across the same point in a future case, he or she is bound by the earlier decision and must decide it in the same way as the earlier judge. This is called a system of "precedent" and results in a build-up of decisions over the years, all of which make up the body of law known as English contract law. When I refer to a case it will generally be in the format A v B (2000) in which A is usually the party who brought the case to court (called the claimant), B is the person against whom the case is being brought (the defendant) and the number in brackets is the year in which the case took place. At the end of the book I have provided a complete list of the cases to which I will refer as I go along.

So let's look at our first case at this point. In the case of *Hyde v Wrench* (1840), Wrench offered to sell his farm to Hyde for £1,000. Hyde counter-offered with a price of £950 which Wrench rejected. The court decided that the counter-offer rejected the original offer so that Hyde could not then accept the original offer of £1,000. Wrench could therefore sell his farm to someone else for a higher price if he so wished.

We can see how this rule can be applied to our situation and the result is that Aaron has rejected Beth's offer to sell the car for £2,100 and has made a counter-offer to buy the car for £1,800.

In actual fact Beth rejects his offer, confident that the car will sell for more than this within a few days. She then offers to sell the car to Aaron for £1,900. However, she quickly reconsiders and before Aaron has a chance to reply, she tells him that she has changed her mind and thinking about it she cannot go below £2,000. She offers to sell the car at that price for cash. Aaron agrees, realising that he isn't going to get the car any cheaper, goes to collect the cash, returns within a couple of hours and pays for the car, having sorted out his insurance cover. He takes the keys and drives the car away.

There are a couple of things to note here. Firstly, we have seen Beth make an offer and then revoke it, albeit very quickly. A person who makes an offer (the offeror, you will recall) is entitled to revoke (that is, withdraw) their offer at any time up until the moment it has been accepted by the person to whom the offer was made (the offeree). This was first decided in the case of *Payne v Cave* (1789). The revocation must be communicated to the offeree. Offers can be revoked even if the offeror had agreed to keep the offer open for a period of time, as seen in the case of *Routledge v Grant* (1828). This is because until the offer is accepted there has been no binding agreement. Beth is therefore free to revoke her offer before Aaron has accepted it, which is what she does.

Secondly, Aaron has accepted Beth's offer. You will recall that acceptance is the second element required for the formation of a contract. Beth made the offer and Aaron accepted it. An acceptance is a clear indication from the offeree that they agree to all the terms of the offer without change (revised terms will constitute a counter-offer). An acceptance is generally seen as effective when it has been successfully communicated to the person who made the offer (the offeror). This rule was confirmed in the case of *Holwell Securities Limited v Hughes* (1974).

In addition to offer and acceptance, the other three elements required in order to form a legally binding contract are consideration, certainty and intention to create a legally binding contract. We can deal with these fairly quickly here, but we will be returning to them as we go through the rest of the book. Consideration is a concept that tends to cause students of law a few problems. It was defined in the case of *Currie v Misa* (1875) as being the benefit or profit gained by one party or the detriment or loss suffered by the other party. Remember, when we refer to a "party", we mean someone who is entering into the contract.

The general rule about consideration is that it must be given by both parties to a contract in order for the contract to be valid. If we look back at our scenario with Aaron and Beth, the final agreement is that Beth will sell her car and Aaron will pay £2,000 for it. Consideration is based on promises. At the time the contract is formed (just before Aaron runs off to get the money), Beth has promised to him that she will sell her car to him for £2,000. Aaron on the other hand has promised to Beth that he will pay £2,000 for the car. Both parties to this contract have therefore provided consideration. Beth's consideration for Aaron's promise is that she will give him the car. Aaron's consideration for Beth's promise is that he will pay her £2,000.

We can see from this that if Beth had promised to give her car to Aaron for free, then that would not constitute a binding contract and Beth could decide not to give the car to Aaron without legal consequences (although once she had given it to him she could not simply take it back). However, if Beth had agreed to sell the car for £500, or £50 or even £5, and Aaron had promised to pay that amount, then there would be a legally binding contract. That is because English law does not assess the commercial validity of the deal that has been agreed. As long as there is consideration being given by each party, the law does not take into account whether that consideration is commercially adequate or not. There are lots of cases on this point, but a well-known one is *Chappell & Co. Ltd v Nestle Co. Ltd* (1960) in which the court decided that even used chocolate wrappers could constitute valid consideration.

Let's move on to certainty. Suffice to say at this point that contract terms need to be certain. That is, they need to be clear and complete. If not, the court may well decide that a contract was never entered into because it is not certain enough as to what the parties were agreeing. As mentioned earlier, you can see why this is more important when things go wrong. If both parties are performing their side of the agreement without problem, then all is well. When they are in dispute, and ask the court to decide who is right, then at that point the court might decide, having considered the terms of the agreement, that those terms are not clear or complete enough for there to be a contract. As I am sure you can imagine, this can leave the parties in a very difficult situation. In the present scenario, the terms are clear and complete. Aaron has agreed to pay £2,000 for the car and Beth has agreed to let him have it immediately. They know which car it is, because it is right in front of them. The only debatable issue could be whether Beth is making any promise about the condition of the car, but it seems like she has not said anything much in this respect and in English law the position is summed up by the Latin phrase "*caveat emptor*" which you may well have come across and which means "let the buyer beware". In other words, subject to any promises made by the seller in this respect, it is up to the buyer to check the condition of what he or she is buying so any risk in that respect falls on Aaron. If the car breaks down before he drives it home, then he will have to sort that out himself without any help from Beth. (The position is different of course when consumers deal with businesses, such as when we buy new goods from high street shops).

Intention is the final element required to form a contract and is the last issue we'll look at in this chapter. Again it can be dealt with fairly quickly here. In order to form a binding contract it is essential that both parties intended to enter into that relationship. When the court considers whether this intention is present, it will look at this from what we call an "objective" standpoint. That means it will look to see whether the parties appeared to intend to be legally bound by their actions when looking in from the outside. It is not a question of asking the parties whether they actually intended to be bound, as it would be too easy for them to deny it if they wanted to escape from their contractual obligations. The court asks itself whether it would be apparent to an independent observer that the parties intended to be bound.

The court has also made good use of a couple of presumptions in the cases that have come before them over the years. The first of these is that in cases which involve social or domestic arrangements, the court will presume that the parties do not intend to be legally bound by their actions. One of the reasons for this is to prevent the courts being filled up with claims about trivial matters. If two friends decide to meet up and go to the cinema, then one cannot sue the other if that other does not turn up as agreed. The court will simply assume that they did not intend to be legally bound by the agreement even though the other elements of a contract (offer, acceptance, consideration and certainty) may be present. A useful example case here is *Balfour v Balfour* (1919) in which the court decided that an agreement between husband and wife was not binding. It is useful to compare this with the case of *Merritt v Merritt* (1970) in which the court decided an agreement was binding when made *after* the marriage had broken down. The presumption that the parties do not intend to create legal relations can be rebutted (overturned), but the courts are reluctant to decide that this has happened except in extreme cases, and often where one party has relied on the agreement, for example, by making significant lifestyle changes.

As you can probably guess, in commercial agreements there is a presumption that the parties did intend to create a legally binding agreement. Again, the courts are very reluctant to displace this presumption. One area where the presumption is often displaced is in relation to claims made in advertisements, especially when it is clear that what is being said is a "joke" or "mere puff" (we'll look at advertisements later in the book). A good example of the presumption being used in a commercial case is *Esso Petroleum Co. Ltd v Commissioners of Customs and Excise* (1976). It is possible to negate the presumption in commercial contracts by expressly stating that the agreement is not binding with clauses such as "subject to contract" or "binding in honour only" which you might have seen on "for sale" boards outside houses or on betting documents such as football pools entry forms.

In the scenario with Aaron and Beth, this would be classed as a commercial situation. Even if they knew each other beforehand, the court would still probably find that they intended to be legally bound. This is a serious matter in which they are buying and selling a car, not a trivial matter. An observer would probably conclude that they intended to be bound by their actions.

This is a good place to end this chapter. We have seen that in order to form a contract there needs to be an offer which is accepted, where both parties are providing some form of consideration, wrapped up in an agreement which has clear and complete terms and where the parties intended to be bound by the agreement. That is what we have with Aaron and Beth and so they have a binding contract. We also covered counter-offers, which bring the current offer to an end and replace it with a new offer, and we also saw how offers can be revoked by the offeror at any stage up to the time of acceptance. Finally, we have introduced ourselves to the courts and the way that previous cases lay down the rules for how future disputes will be decided. I promise that we will be covering much of this information again, so even if you have not grasped everything first time, please keep reading…!

Chapter 3 – Adverts and other things

In the last chapter we saw how Aaron and Beth entered into a contract "face to face" after Aaron had chanced upon a car for sale and decided to enter into negotiations with Beth. In this chapter I want to look at several fairly common scenarios which all beg the question "Has there been an offer?"

The first situation, and the most common, is that of advertisements. Many adverts, including television and radio adverts, advertising hoardings, leaflets, posters, websites and so on, contain statements which could look like offers. Some may even use the word "offer". However, there is a practical problem with classing such things as offers. If the advertiser was deemed to be making an offer, then they would potentially be legally bound to sell to every person who accepted that offer. This means that the seller would need to have unlimited stocks of the product, or the means to provide an unlimited amount of the service, which is being advertised. Due to this "limited stocks" problem, in law an advert is classed as an "invitation to treat". This rather peculiar phrase means that the seller is not deemed to be making an offer, but is inviting other people to make an offer, which the seller can then either accept or reject in the usual way. This leaves control of the transaction in the hands of the advertiser. When stocks are gone, all subsequent offers can simply be rejected. Adverts often state "Whilst Stocks Last" or "Subject To Availability" just to make sure this point is clear. A legal case which supports this idea is *Partridge v Crittenden* (1968), which is easy to remember because it was about an advertisement for the sale of birds, although not Partridges! The court said that this was an invitation to treat and therefore did not amount to an offer for sale (which would have been a criminal offence on the particular facts).

Beth could have advertised her car in the local newspaper safe in the knowledge that she would not have been bound to sell to anyone in particular. People responding to the advert would have been making offers to her and she could accept or reject them as she wanted to. Of course, any offer received would still need to fulfil the requirements of an offer in that it would need to set out the terms on which the offeror was willing to be bound and it would need to be communicated to Beth.

What Beth actually did of course was to display the car "for sale" on her driveway. Goods are sold in this way all the time. Think about a display of goods in a shop. Again the courts have held that this kind of arrangement is an invitation to treat and not an offer. Therefore a shop is not offering to sell you the goods in the store, however strange that may sound. The shop is simply asking you to make it an offer, and suggesting a price at which it will probably be willing to sell. The court has decided that in fact the customer makes the offer by taking the goods to the checkout and handing them to the checkout assistant. The shop can then decide whether to accept or reject the offer. This was decided in the case of *Pharmaceutical Society of Great Britain v Boots Cash Chemists (Southern) Limited* (1952). The point at which the sale was made was important because the sale of certain products had to be supervised by a registered pharmacist. This happened at the checkout and so Boots were not guilty of any offence.

By displaying her car, Beth was not therefore offering it for sale, but inviting others to make her an offer.

We'll cover a couple of other situations here although these are a little more specialist in nature. The first of these is a request for tenders. A request for tenders is where a person asks others to provide a detailed quotation for a particular job and then selects the best quotation received, however that may be judged. For example, a local authority might decide that it wants to put its refuse collection out to tender. In other words, ask for offers or bids from interested companies detailing how they would provide the service and at what cost to the local authority. Once received, the local authority can then assess which offer it prefers and it will then accept that offer. As you can probably guess from the process, a request for tenders is therefore an invitation to treat and the bids are offers which can then be accepted or rejected as desired. This was exemplified in the case of *Spencer v Harding* (1870). Having said that, it is worth noting that a request for tenders can lead to an obligation to actually consider (though not accept) any tenders which are submitted in accordance with the terms of the request. This was decided in *Blackpool and Fylde Aero Club Limited v Blackpool Borough Council* (1990).

The final subject for this chapter is the auction. Of course, Beth could have sold her car at a car auction. An auction is run by an auctioneer who sells items on behalf of other people. Beth would put her car into an auction and the auctioneer would invite people to make bids for the car. The car would be sold to the highest bidder. The general position, as I am sure you will be unsurprised to discover, is that the request for bids by the auctioneer is an invitation to treat. The bids themselves are then offers to buy and the auctioneer can accept or reject as they choose. This was decided in the case of *Payne v Cave* (1789) (we've seen this case before as it is also a case which decided that an offer can be withdrawn at any point up to acceptance). The fall of the auctioneer's hammer signifies the end of the auction and the point at which the highest bid is accepted by the auctioneer and the binding contract formed.

We've looked at some fairly common scenarios in this chapter – advertisements, displays of goods, requests for tenders and auction sales. We've seen that all are generally classed in law as invitations to treat, so that the person responding to the advert, display or request is the person who makes the offer and the person who placed the advert, or made the display or request can either accept or reject the offer in the usual way. Alternatively, they could of course enter into negotiations with that person, as indeed Beth did with Aaron when he saw her display of goods (the car).

Chapter 4 – Unilateral contracts

Let's start this chapter with a word of warning. The unilateral contract is something which seems to cause students of law many problems. In fact they are quite rare and are reasonably straightforward, but due to the emphasis placed on them when learning about the rules of contract law, students often try to apply the rules about unilateral contracts to situations which simply do not merit it.

So what is a unilateral contract? Well, there are two basic types of contract, called bilateral contracts and unilateral contracts. The vast majority of contracts entered into are bilateral contracts. As usual, "bi" here means two. A bilateral contract is a contract in which both parties promise to do something. If we think once again back to Aaron and Beth and the sale of the car, we can see that they entered into a bilateral contract. That is because they both made a promise to each other. Aaron promised to pay £2,000 for the car and Beth promised to hand over the car to Aaron. You can probably see how this will apply to most contracts. One party usually agrees to supply some item or service in return for an amount of money. One party promises to provide the item or service and the other party promises to pay for it. This is true even in those situations where the transaction happens immediately. When I approach a shop checkout and hand my goods to the checkout assistant, I am offering to buy them and the assistant will accept my offer by taking my money. I am promising to pay and then I do pay, and the assistant (on behalf of the shop) is promising to supply the goods to me and then does supply them to me. This all happens very quickly but it is nonetheless a bilateral contract in which both parties have made a promise.

A unilateral contract is therefore one in which only one party makes a promise. The best way to understand this is to look at an example. Let's assume my dog runs away when we are out for a walk in the local park. I look for it and call its name but it does not return. I decide that the best thing to do is to put a notice on the lamppost at the entrance to the park. This notice includes a description and a picture of my dog with my telephone number and a promise of a reward of £50 for the person who returns the dog to me.

This notice is likely to constitute a unilateral offer. When this is accepted it will form a unilateral contract. It is unilateral because I am the only one who is making a promise here. No one is promising to find my dog, but if they do, I am promising to pay a £50 reward if they return the dog to me. I do not expect anyone to telephone me and explain that they have accepted my offer and are now going out to find the dog. If they did, they could potentially be legally bound to find the dog, all of which is a little nonsensical. Instead, people look at the notice and as they continue to do whatever it is they are doing in the park, they perhaps keep an eye open for any stray dogs. If they happen to find my dog, and they decide to get hold of it and telephone me and then bring the dog to my address then so be it, but they don't have to do that because they haven't promised to do so.

However, I have made a promise to them, and if they do decide to bring the dog to my house, then at that point they have accepted my offer and I am legally bound to pay them the £50 reward. At any time up to that point they could decide not to return the dog to me and I would not have to pay the reward. I made a unilateral offer which became a unilateral contract when the other person accepted my offer. They accepted it not by telling me that they have accepted, but by performing the act which I requested in my offer (returning my dog).

The leading case on unilateral contracts and one of the best known contract law cases generally is *Carlill v Carbolic Smoke Ball Co.* (1893). Mrs Carlill purchased a smoke ball which was advertised as being a defence against influenza. She used the smoke ball as directed and then caught influenza. The original advertisement said that anyone who did this would be paid compensation of £100. The court decided that the advertisement was more than just an advertisement and amounted to a unilateral offer to anyone who saw it. The terms of that offer were that anyone who used the smoke ball properly and then caught influenza could claim the £100 compensation. That is what Mrs Carlill did. Obviously she never made any promises about catching influenza. This was a unilateral offer by the Smoke Ball Co. and Mrs Carlill fulfilled the terms of that offer. By doing so, she accepted the offer (in the same way as the finder of my lost dog) and became entitled to the "reward". The original advertisement said that the company had put aside £1,000 into a separate bank account as evidence of their good will and the court found this persuasive in deciding that the advertisement amounted to an offer. Of course, this does not mean that advertisements generally are offers. We know that they are invitations to treat. But it does show that it is possible to turn them into offers if the wording is very precise about the terms of the offer.

Unilateral contracts give rise to several issues which we ought to consider here briefly for completeness. Firstly, you can see from the above that acceptance of the offer does not need to be communicated in quite the same way as for a "normal" offer. However, it is worth noting that the acceptance (performance of the act) must be in response to the offer. In other words, to accept it the person must know about the offer. If someone finds my dog and returns it to me without knowing about the offer of the reward, then I do not need to pay the reward, however mean that may seem!

Secondly, revoking (or withdrawing) a unilateral offer can cause problems. Such offers are often made to the whole world; my lost dog notice is made to anyone who reads it for example. It is generally accepted that the effective way to withdraw a unilateral offer is to use the same means as was used to make the offer in the first place. If I have made a unilateral offer on a poster outside my house, then I should use the same means to tell people that the offer has been revoked, on the basis presumably that the same people who saw the offer are likely to see the revocation.

Another problem with revoking a unilateral contract is that generally we have seen that an offer can be revoked at any time up until it has been accepted. If acceptance of a unilateral offer takes place only when full performance is complete, then I could revoke my offer at the last minute, when performance has almost been completed but not quite. This could cause hardship on the person performing the act. It is with this in mind that in the case of *Errington v Errington and*

Woods (1952) the court decided that a unilateral contract could not be revoked once performance had begun.

In this chapter we have looked at unilateral contracts. Remember that these are not very common. Most contracts are bilateral in nature as both parties are promising to do something. Unilateral contracts give rise to some interesting issues such as acceptance and revocation, and therefore tend to attract a lot of coverage in contract law books. However, try not to over-estimate their importance in the real world.

Chapter 5 – Some practical things

In this chapter I want to mention a few areas which are relevant to the topics we have already covered but which I have not specifically referred to so far. They include the postal rule of acceptance, the "battle of forms" and electronic commerce (e-commerce).

You will recall that the basic rule on acceptance is that it operates only when it is received by the person who made the original offer (the offeror). This basic rule makes good sense because if I want to accept an offer the onus is placed on me to ensure that I use a reliable means of communication to indicate my acceptance of the offer to the offeror. If there is a chance that my acceptance will not reach the offeror then the risk falls on me in that no contract is formed in that case and my acceptance fails.

The postal rule of acceptance was established in the case of *Adams v Lindsell* (1818). In this case, the court decided that where the post is used to make an acceptance, then the acceptance can take effect from the time it is posted rather than when it is received. In other words, the usual rule for the timing of an acceptance is displaced. Like unilateral contracts, this is another area which attracts quite a lot of consideration in law books and which is not nearly so important in the real world of contract law. This rule should be considered in the light of the age of the case which created it. In the early 19th century the post was the most common form of communication and so rules had to be created to account for the vagaries of the postal system. The thought was that the person making the offer should be expecting some form of reply and was therefore in a better position to make enquiries if no response came. The postal rule means that the offeror could be bound to a contract despite not having received any acceptance from the other person (the offeree).

In practice, the post is not used so often these days although many important contracts still require a physical signature and so it is certainly not irrelevant. It is entirely possible for the offeror to state in the offer itself that any acceptance will not be operational until it has been received by the offeror, and the courts will be quick to recognise any attempt to do this as excluding the operation of the postal rule.

One other thing to remember here is that the postal rule only applies to acceptance, not to anything else such as the making of an offer or a counter-offer, or a revocation (withdrawing the offer) or a rejection, which are all subject to the usual rule that they must be communicated to be effective.

Whilst on the subject of acceptance, we should also mention here that silence cannot be deemed to be acceptance. I cannot make you an offer and state that if I hear nothing from you then I will assume the offer is accepted. This would result in nuisance offers being made which require some positive action to reject them to avoid the assumption of acceptance by silence. The rule stems from the case of *Felthouse v Bindley* (1862).

Another practical aspect of what we have looked at so far is known as the "battle of forms". What we mean by this becomes clearer if we think how contracts are formed in the commercial world. Very often an order for goods or services will be sent to another business together with a set of standard terms and conditions of purchase which will form an offer. Rather than accepting that offer, the other business may well reply by sending its own terms and conditions of sale. As these terms and conditions will be different, they will constitute a counter offer which, as we know, rejects the original offer and replaces it with a new offer. The original company (the buyer) may well acknowledge receipt by re-sending its own terms and conditions of purchase which again will be a counter offer. This could continue for some time until eventually the goods are delivered (possibly with yet another copy of the terms and conditions of the seller enclosed).

The terms and conditions are what is meant by the "forms". The "battle" is about whose terms and conditions finally apply to the sale of the goods, hence the term "battle of forms". It is an important point because the two sets of terms and conditions will be significantly different. In a dispute, the difficult task of the court is to determine what, if any, terms are included in the contract. The most well-known case on this subject is *Butler Machine Tool Co. Limited v Ex-Cell-O Corporation (England) Limited* (1979). The court decided that it must use the traditional offer and acceptance approach to this situation and therefore it will look to see which set of terms and conditions arrived last and was finally accepted by the other side. That acceptance is often done by conduct (for example, by delivering or accepting delivery of the goods in question).

The final area I want to cover here is that of e-commerce. There are some special rules and regulations that apply to such things (which are beyond the scope of this book) but generally the normal rules of contract apply. So, for example, two people negotiating over a contract by e-mail and then agreeing the terms of a contract by e-mail are really just doing the same as they would if they were sat face to face. Contracts do not have to be in written form. We make contracts all the time by speaking to someone (for example, when buying goods over the telephone or even in a shop). E-mail is a form of written communication and follows the normal rules of contract. Similarly, when we buy things through a website, the website is really just an electronic advertisement, or an electronic shop display which will constitute an invitation to treat. The user of the website then makes an order (an offer) which is usually then "accepted" by some automatic process.

Interesting questions arise about e-commerce such as whether the postal rule of acceptance applies to electronic mail, or whether the acceptance of an order by a website is only effective when it has been received by the customer.

The purpose of this chapter was really just to highlight some areas which were not covered in the first few chapters but which are relevant to those issues. They are topics which you will read more about if you continue your interest in contract law beyond a basic introductory book of this nature.

Chapter 6 – Consideration

The first few chapters have focused on how to form a contract and in particular the need for an offer and an acceptance leading to an agreement. We also saw that the parties must be clear about the terms on which they are contracting and also that they must intend to be legally bound. In addition we touched on the need for both parties to provide consideration, and this chapter will look at this issue in more detail.

Let's remind ourselves what we mean by consideration. We said that consideration is a concept that tends to cause some confusion for students new to the study of English contract law. It was defined in the case of *Currie v Misa* (1875) as being the benefit or profit gained by one party or the detriment or loss suffered by the other party. A slightly more modern definition was approved of in the case of *Dunlop Pneumatic Tyre Co Limited v Selfridge & Co Limited* (1915), which more clearly expressed consideration as being the "price" paid for the other party's promise.

All of this means that both parties to a contract must provide something of value in the eyes of the law. This could be something of benefit to the other party or something of detriment to themselves, and which is given in return for the promise made by the other party. This caused no problems with Aaron and Beth as the consideration was clear. Aaron was paying £2,000 and this would be of benefit to Beth (she receives it) and of detriment to Aaron (he loses it). Similarly, Beth is passing ownership in her car to Aaron, so he benefits by receiving the car and she suffers a detriment by losing the car. Both have therefore clearly provided consideration for the other's promise.

We also saw earlier that a court will not assess whether the consideration is legally adequate, only that some consideration does actually exist. A mismatch in the value of the consideration being provided does not in itself make the contract invalid. If I agree to sell my house for £10 then that is up to me and the court will enforce the contract as long as it is clear that I intended to be legally bound and that I was mentally competent and had not been defrauded. However, we also saw that if I agreed to give my house away for free, then the court will not enforce that agreement because the person to whom I am giving the house has not provided any consideration.

Another principle of consideration which we will cover here is the idea that past consideration cannot be valid consideration. In other words, a promise made in respect of an act which has already been performed will not give rise to a legally enforceable obligation. For example, if Beth agreed to give her car to Aaron and then did actually give her car to Aaron, and then later Aaron promised to pay her £500 for her generosity, his promise would not be enforceable by Beth because Beth did not provide anything in exchange – the gift of the car had already taken place. A good example case is *Roscorla v Thomas* (1842) where a warranty (a promise as to the quality of something) was given after the contract had been agreed. The court found that the warranty came too late to be counted as consideration for the purchaser's promise to pay the price and therefore not enforceable.

Another general principle about consideration is that an obligation to a person to perform an existing contractual duty cannot be consideration for a further promise from the same person. This is probably best explained using an example. The best known case is *Stilk v Myrick* (1809). That case involved a crew member of a ship who had agreed to sail the ship to its destination and back. At some point on the voyage a couple of other crew members deserted the ship. The captain promised an additional payment to the crew member if he agreed to continue with the voyage despite the loss of the other two crew members. Once the ship was back in port the captain refused to pay. The court decided that the crew member had done no more than he had originally agreed to do. That was, sail the ship to its destination and back again. Since he had done nothing "new" he had therefore not provided any consideration for the extra payment offered by the captain and so the "additional" agreement was not binding. The crew member was only due his basic payment, not the extra payment.

Whilst this case must be seen in its historical context (the court not wanting to encourage crew members to hold the captain to ransom when at sea), and it is true that the courts take a more relaxed view of this principle in modern times, the general rule is still valid. To alter the terms of an existing contract (which is what this basically amounts to), new consideration needs to be provided by both parties.

For completeness here, it is worth mentioning that an existing duty to *someone else* can constitute valid consideration for a further contractual promise to another person. For example, if I agree with one person to clear the snow from a shared car park outside a block of flats in return for payment, then I can enter into similar separate agreements with each of the other occupants, despite the fact that I am performing the same task (the same consideration) in relation to each agreement.

This chapter has focused on the topic of consideration because it tends to be quite a difficult concept for those who are new to the study of English contract law. We have seen that it is the benefit provided or the detriment suffered by each party to the contract. We have seen that it needs to be something of value, but need not be of adequate or equivalent commercial value to the consideration provided by the other party to the contract. We have also seen that consideration provided in the past cannot be valid consideration for a new contract, and neither can an existing contractual duty owed to the person with whom I am now contracting.

Chapter 7 – The end of an offer

This will be a short chapter which just clarifies the ways in which an offer can come to an end. We have in fact already looked at a couple of them. We saw earlier how the person who made the offer (the offeror) can revoke (withdraw) the offer at any time up to the point of its acceptance. We noted that the postal rule does not apply to revocation by post, so that a revocation is only effective when notified to the offeree. However, this notification can come from any reliable source, not just from the offeror. This point was seen to operate in the case of *Dickinson v Dodds* (1876). In that case the fact that a house, which was the subject of an offer between the parties, had been sold to someone else was communicated to the offeree by someone other than the offeror, and the court decided that this amounted to a valid revocation of the original offer.

We have also looked at counter-offers which were made in the course of negotiations between Aaron and Beth about the car. You will recall that a counter-offer is a response which changes the terms of the original offer in some way and therefore operates as a rejection of that offer, replacing it with a new offer made by the person to whom the original offer was made.

This brings us nicely to rejection generally. Obviously, an offer can be brought to an end by a simple outright rejection. There is nothing contentious about this point.

A final way for an offer to come to an end is by lapse of time. If an offer is not rejected or revoked, and no counter-offer is received, for how long will that offer be open for the offeree to accept it? Clearly it will not simply stand as an offer forever. The answer here is that the offer will stay open for a "reasonable time". What is reasonable will depend on the facts of each individual case. Offers in relation to complex deals or valuable items may well be deemed to remain "alive" for longer than more straightforward offers. In the case of *Ramsgate Victoria Hotel Co v Montefiore* (1866), the court decided that six months was too long for an offer to be left hanging before it was accepted. The offer related to the purchase of company shares.

It is possible for the offeror to set a time limit for the offer, so that the offer will expire if not accepted within the time limit. It is worth noting however, that even if an offeror agrees specifically to keep an offer open for a set period of time, the offeror can still revoke the offer within that time because the agreement to keep the offer open is generally not binding. The position is different if the offeree has given some consideration for the promise by the offeror to keep the offer open, for example, by paying a sum of money to the offeror.

    This chapter has summarised the ways in which an offer can be brought to an end, the main methods being rejection, counter-offer, revocation and lapse of time.

Chapter 8 – The terms of a contract

We saw earlier in the book that the terms of a contract must be clear and complete. They should be set out in the offer and accepted without amendment by the offeree. The terms of a contract do not need to be written down but if they are then it is obviously much easier to determine what those terms are. Contracts are entered into all the time without the terms being written down and these are still valid contracts, but it can then be more difficult to establish exactly what the terms of the contract are.

One thing that needs to be distinguished from a term of the contract is a representation. This is a statement of fact which helps to induce or encourage the other person to enter into the contract, but which does not in itself become a term of the contract. If that statement turns out to be false, then the maker of the statement has potentially made a misrepresentation, which is a topic that we will look at in more detail in Chapter 14.

For now, it is important to be able to determine what is a term of the contract and what is merely a representation. If something is a term of the contract then if it turns out to be false, or if it is a promise which is not performed properly, it will give rise to what we call a breach of contract. Again, we will look at the effects of this later in the book, in Chapters 12 and 13, but because a breach of contract is treated differently from a misrepresentation, it is important to be able to tell the two things apart.

Let's assume that Aaron decided not to buy Beth's car. He is now browsing through the local newspaper and sees an advert for "Carl's Cars" which includes photographs of several cars with prices printed across them. Aaron likes the look of a small red hatchback, not unlike the one that Beth was selling, but cheaper at £1,600. Of course, Aaron needs to remember that an advertisement is not generally classed as an offer, and so he cannot guarantee that he will get the car for that price. It may already be sold of course, and even if it is still for sale, the advertisement is an invitation to treat which is inviting Aaron to make an offer for the car. He is probably safe to assume that if he offered £1,600 the seller would accept his offer, but there is no guarantee of that.

Aaron arrives at Carl's Cars and a man in a suit comes out to greet him and introduces himself as Carl. Aaron explains that he has seen an advertisement wants to know a bit more about the car. How do we know whether the statements made by Carl are representations, or terms of the contract (if they enter into a contract for the purchase of the car)?

One test used by the courts is whether the maker of the statement knew the facts; whether he or she was an expert in the field, for example. In the case of *Oscar Chess Limited v Williams* (1957) the court decided that a person selling a car who was not an expert only made a representation when they stated the age of the car based on the car's registration document. In fact the car was ten years older than he stated and therefore worth a lot less than he sold it for. Had a car dealer made the same statement, it would probably be a term of the contract because we would expect that person to know the facts. This can be seen in the case of *Dick Bentley Productions Limited v Harold Smith (Motors) Limited* (1965). The contractual term would be about the age of the car. Anyone listening to the statement would assume it was true, whereas anyone listening to the seller in the *Oscar Chess* case might well think that the seller does not know the facts and therefore cannot be offering that fact as a contractual term.

Another test used by the courts to determine whether a statement is a term of the contract or a representation is the significance of the statement to the recipient. In the case of *Bannerman v White* (1861) the buyer wanted to know that the hops were free from sulphur. The court decided that the seller's statement to that effect was a term of the contract because the buyer had indicated how important that fact was to his decision to buy the hops.

Finally here, if there has been a long period between the statement and the actual formation of the contract then the court may well decide that the statement is a representation. The nearer the statement occurs to the point of formation, then the more likely it will be a term of the contract which is then entered into. This can be seen in the case of *Routledge v McKay* (1954).

So to answer our question about which statements made by Carl will become terms of the contract with Aaron, the answer is probably that some of them will, if they are statements of fact, because he is an "expert" in selling cars. Certainly anything which Aaron asks and highlights as being particularly important to him will likely become a term of the contract. If they enter into a written contract then this will of course determine what the "terms" are. Anything left out at this stage is likely to be just a representation.

So far we have looked at the question of whether a particular statement is a term of the contract or not. If we decide it is a representation, then it is not a term and so therefore not included in the contract. If the statement turns out to be false, then it might constitute a misrepresentation and we will cover that later in Chapter 14. We now need to think about how terms can be incorporated into a contract.

The most obvious way to incorporate a term into a contract is for the contract to be written out and signed by both parties. If someone signs a written contract, then as long as no fraud has taken place, they are bound by the terms of the contract even if they have not read it.

However, most contracts are not made in writing. In that case, the key thing to remember is that terms can only be incorporated if they are added *before* the contract is finalised.

It is fair to say that the question of whether a term has been successfully incorporated or not arises most commonly in relation to exclusion clauses. An exclusion clause is a contractual clause which tries to exclude liability for breach of contract. We will therefore continue our discussion of incorporation of terms later in Chapter 15 when we talk about exclusion clauses in more detail.

For the remainder of this chapter I want to look at the situation when the terms of a contract are not clear or complete. The position of unclear terms is that the court will try its best to interpret the clauses as a reasonable person would understand them to read, having regard to anything available to the parties which might influence this understanding. This point comes from the case of *Investors Compensation Scheme Limited v West Bromwich Building Society* (1998). In other words the court looks at the meaning of the clauses from the standpoint of a "mythical" reasonable person, rather than looking at what the parties to the contract actually meant. This is because it is all too easy for the parties to turn round later and claim that the clauses did not reflect their actual intentions.

If the court decides that the clauses are not clear enough to determine what the parties must have intended, then it can simply decide that the contract is unenforceable, as seen in *Scammell and Nephew Limited v Ouston* (1941). In that case a contract for sale on "hire purchase terms" was simply not clear enough as there are numerous different types of hire purchase (where a "buyer" hires an asset such as a car for a period of time and then purchases it (or has the option to purchase it) at the end of the period).

When it comes to incomplete contracts again the court can decide that the missing parts are fatal to the existence of a valid contract and declare that there is no enforceable contract. However, it also has several ways of implying terms into contracts. What we mean by implying a term is that the courts try to work out what is missing based on what a reasonable person would think the parties to the contract intended to agree. So what methods are open to the court to do this?

One thing the court can do is to look at any customs or trade practices in the particular field in which the parties are operating. For example, in *British Crane Hire Corporation Limited v Ipswich Plant Hire Limited* (1975), the court decided that the contract between the parties included terms from a standard form of contract widely used in the particular trade and which both parties would have been familiar with.

Another tool that the courts have to complete a contract is to consider what terms would give effect to the parties' intentions as viewed from an objective standpoint. We have encountered this word before and we saw that it means from the point of view of someone looking into the transaction from the outside, not the actual intentions of the actual parties. In other words, the courts try to establish what the parties appeared to intend form their words and actions. The case law in this area is complex but the courts will generally only imply terms into a contract where it is necessary to reflect the apparent intentions of the parties and to make the contract work. A well-known example is the case of *The Moorcock* (1889). The owner of a wharf on the river Thames agreed to allow the owner of a boat to unload at the wharf. Both were aware that the ship would settle on the riverbed at low tide, but it settled onto hard ground and was damaged. The court decided that there was an implied term in the contract that the boat would settle onto soft ground as otherwise the contract was simply not workable. Therefore, the owner of the wharf was liable for the damage to the boat even though the contract itself was silent on the matter.

Sometimes the court decides that a contract of a particular type should have certain terms implied into it, on the basis that those terms are a necessary feature of that type of contract. For example, in the case of *Liverpool City Council v Irwin* (1977), the court decided that, in a contract for the lease of a flat in a block of flats with shared use of common areas such as lifts and stairways, there is an implied term that the landlord will take reasonable care to maintain those areas. This has the effect of implying this term into all similar contracts where such matters have not specifically been covered by the express contractual terms.

One final area worth a mention in this chapter is that terms can be implied by statute. We mentioned statutes briefly earlier in the book as being law made by the UK Parliament. They are basically legal rules written out as numbered lists on various topics. We said that most law is created in this way and that contract law was exceptional in that it has been created mainly by a series of case decisions. We have referred to examples of those decisions as we have gone through the book. However, there are some statutes relevant to contract law and a couple of important examples are the Sale of Goods Act 1979 and the Consumer Rights Act 2015. If I buy something in a shop it would be unusual for me to enter into a written contract. However, if the item I purchased, say a television, did not work properly, then I might expect to get my money back or at least be entitled to have the item repaired. If I have not entered into a written contract and presumably said very little about contractual terms at the time of purchase, then where do I get my rights from? The answer is from the Consumer Rights Act and similar statutes. The Act implies certain terms into "consumer" contracts to protect the consumer. A consumer is someone who is buying other than in a business capacity. So for example, the Act would imply terms about the quality of the product I have purchased and the fitness for its usual purpose. If my television turns out to be faulty, then I can use these provisions to obtain a refund or a repair. Similar terms are implied into business contracts by the Sale of Goods Act 1979, and excluding their operation can be difficult if not impossible, as we'll see later in Chapter 15.

In this chapter we have considered the difference between contractual terms and representations, and looked at how terms can be implied into contracts to fill any gaps.

Chapter 9 – Discharge of contractual liability

The obligations that two parties owe to each other under a contract can come to an end in a variety of ways. The most obvious is by performance of those obligations in accordance with the contract. If I employ a decorator to paint my dining room, then the contract will come to a natural end when the decorator has finished painting my dining room to an acceptable standard and I have paid the money I owe under the contract. The obligations that we both had have been performed as envisaged in our contract and so it has now ended.

Another way that the contract may come to an end is by agreement. This could be before performance has started. For example, if the decorator telephones me to say that he is not very well and will not be able to complete the job for a few weeks, then we may agree to release each other from our respective obligations. I agree that he does not need to decorate my dining room and he agrees that I do not need to pay him. By releasing each other in this way, we have both effectively provided consideration for our "new" agreement not to hold each other to the contractual obligations in the original contract.

The other two main methods by which a contract is discharged are through "frustration" and "breach". They are the subjects of Chapters 10 and 12 respectively. We'll look at what happens when the parties make a mistake in Chapter 11 because this sits well with the concept of frustration.

Chapter 10 – Frustration

A contract becomes frustrated when it becomes impossible to perform or when performance becomes something very different to what was envisaged when the contract was entered into. Generally the circumstance which alters things must be something which was outside the control of the contracting parties.

The common example used to explain frustration is the case of *Taylor v Caldwell* (1863). In that case an agreement for the hire of a concert hall was frustrated when the concert hall burnt down in a fire which was not the fault of either party to the contract. You can see that the contract could no longer be performed as agreed because the concert hall no longer existed.

It is important to note that if an obligation under a contract has become more difficult to perform this will not usually give rise to frustration. So, for example, a shortage of skilled workers in the case of *Davis Contractors Limited v Fareham UDC* (1956) did not result in frustration; the contract could still be performed and the shortage should have been provided for in the contract.

Other examples of contracts that would be frustrated include where the contract becomes illegal to perform (perhaps due to some change in the law which occurs after the contract is entered into) and also where the purpose of the contract is frustrated. This latter point can be seen in the well-known case of *Krell v Henry* (1903). A room was hired out to view the coronation procession of Edward VII which was then cancelled. The court agreed that both parties knew that viewing the procession was the main reason for the contract and so decided it was frustrated. It is important to note that the purpose must be known to both parties and be a key reason for the contract. The fact that a football match is cancelled in London would not allow me to claim that my contract with the train company is frustrated; the train company generally has no knowledge of why I am travelling to London.

In actual fact commercial contracts will often provide for many potentially frustrating events, so that the contract will govern what is to happen if, for example, part of a contract becomes impossible to perform. In this way the parties can decide between themselves, as part of their contractual negotiations, who will be "at risk" if such an event occurs. Suitable insurance can then be arranged where possible.

However, it is worth a quick look at what happens when a contract is frustrated and the parties have not provided for it in their contract. When that happens, the general position is that all contractual obligations automatically come to an end. Historically this could have harsh consequences. Lucky timing often played a key role; you might have paid for something and not received it, in which case you would never receive it. Or you might have received something and not paid for it, in which case you would not have to pay for it. This probably over-simplifies the position, but in any case those rules have been replaced by another piece of legislation. The Law Reform (Frustrated Contracts) Act 1943 provides that money payable in advance under the contract is recoverable by the person who paid it, and money due to be paid but not yet paid is no longer payable. However, the Act also gives the court discretion to allow the recipient of any advance payment to retain some of that payment if it is fair in the circumstances. Similarly, the court can allow the potential recipient of any money due under the contract to claim such proportion of that money as the court thinks is fair in the circumstances.

In addition, the Act provides that where one party has in some way performed their side of the contract and has, by doing that, conferred some valuable benefit on the other party, the court has discretion to award the performing party such sum as it considers just. Note that this is not about incurring expenses; there must be something of value which the other party is "paying" for.

We have seen in this chapter that contracts can be frustrated by events occurring which are generally beyond the control of the parties. They are often unexpected or unforeseen. The contract is brought to an end by frustration and the implications of this are governed by the Law Reform (Frustrated Contracts) Act 1943. Important contracts usually have some provision in them to cover the position.

Chapter 11 – Mistake

If a mistake is made in a written contract which results in the written version of the agreement not reflecting what was actually agreed between the parties, then the court can be asked to grant an order for rectification. This will have the effect of amending the written contract as necessary to reflect the original intentions of the parties.

However we are concerned with different types of mistake in this chapter. For example, what if I contract to sell something to a buyer who turns out not to be the person they claimed to be? What if I contract to buy something which, unbeknown to either me or the seller, has already been destroyed? I'm sure you can think of other examples of this kind of mistake. So what effect does this have, if any, on the contract?

We can split the issue into two areas. The first includes those mistakes which are made when forming the contract so that despite the parties appearing to have reached an agreement, in fact they never did and so no contract has been formed. The second covers those situations where the parties are both labouring under the same mistake, so that they have in fact reached agreement but not in the way that they intended.

Mistakes made on formation include the situation where the parties both make a mistake or where one party makes a mistake. The court must then decide which interpretation of the situation is more reasonable. A good example is the case of *Smith v Hughes* (1871) in which the seller was selling "new oats" and the buyer wanted to buy "old oats". They entered into a contract and then realised that the buyer had bought the "wrong kind" of oats. The court decided that the seller's interpretation was the most reasonable in that this was a sale of oats, and it was up to the buyer to ensure they were suitable for his purposes. The contract was therefore valid and the buyer had to pay up.

Another example of a mistake which can occur as the contract is formed is that of mistaken identity. The courts have had great difficulty in reaching a clear and satisfactory answer to the problem which arises when a person deals with a fraudster. If a jeweller sells an expensive item on credit to someone who she believes is a well-known celebrity, but that person turns out to be a fraudster, then a problem arises. The fraudster is likely to sell the item on to an innocent third party for cash. If the fraudster cannot be traced, then one of the innocent parties will lose out (either the jeweller or the eventual buyer), but the law has a dilemma as to who that should be. If the transaction remains valid, then the jeweller has lost an item for which she will never be paid. If the transaction is cancelled, the eventual innocent buyer will have paid for an item which he will have to return to the jeweller. The fraudster, in either event, gets to keep the money received from the sale of the item to the third party.

We tend to find that if the contract is in writing, then the courts presume that the seller intended to deal with the named person. This can be seen in operation in the case of *Shogan Finance Limited v Norman Hudson* (2002). As the actual buyer is a fraudster and not the named buyer, then the contract is void and the ownership of the goods being sold remains with the seller. In that case, the innocent eventual buyer must return the goods. This is also the case where the identity of the buyer is of fundamental importance.

If the contract is not in writing, then the court tends to decide that the seller intended to contract with the actual physical person standing in front of them, in other words the fraudster. This situation occurred in the case of *Lewis v Avery* (1972). In that case the contract stood and the innocent eventual buyer could keep the goods and the seller lost out.

Let's now look at situations where the parties appear to have reached an agreement but it turns out that they were both labouring under the same mistake, so that they have in fact reached agreement but not in the way that they intended. This often concerns the existence or quality of the thing that they were contracting about. The courts are reluctant to allow such claims due to the potential effects on innocent third parties. However, a good example of when a claim for mistake will be allowed is the case of *Couturier v Hastie* (1856). In that case, the owner of come corn agreed to sell it to the buyer when unbeknown to both of them it had already been sold on the buyer's behalf. The court agreed that the contract was void for mistake, meaning the seller did not have to sell the corn and the buyer had no obligation to pay for it.

When it comes to a mistake as to the quality of the goods, the court is reluctant to interfere with the agreement of the parties. One of the most well-known cases here is *Leaf v International Galleries* (1950) which involved an agreement to sell a painting by the famous artist Constable. In fact it was discovered five years later that it was not painted by Constable, but the court decided that this was simply a mistake as to quality; the parties had still sold and purchased the exact painting they thought they were dealing with, it was just not of the same quality that they thought it was. In other words, the contract could still be (and had been) completed as agreed.

We have seen in this chapter that the principle of contractual mistake is a complex and rather unsatisfactory topic. Mistakes have to be important in order for the court to allow the contract to be made void. They might do this where the subject matter no longer exists for example. They are unlikely to do it where the subject matter is not of the same quality as the parties thought it was. We have also seen that the court is more likely to allow the contract to be made void in written contractual agreements than in face to face dealings.

Chapter 12 – Breach of contract

Davina runs her own bakery business and contacts Ed, a local ingredient supplier. He offers to supply ingredients to Davina on the first working day of each month for the next 12 months for a fixed price of £300 per month, payable within seven days of each delivery. Davina agrees with these terms and so accepts his offer.

As a reminder, this amounts to a valid contract. Ed made an offer containing the terms of the contract, which Davina accepted. The terms were certain (let's assume the detail of what exactly was being delivered was agreed), and both parties clearly provided the necessary consideration; Ed has promised to deliver baking ingredients, and Davina has promised to pay £300 for them each month. There is also an intention to create legal relations. This is a business or commercial transaction and therefore a court would assume that the parties intended to be legally bound by their actions.

Everything goes to plan for the first three months of the contract which sees Ed deliver good quality produce and Davina paid for them as agreed. However, in the fourth month Ed's delivery is a few days late. Davina agrees to overlook this and pays for the ingredients as usual. On the fifth month, Ed's delivery is three weeks late and Davina is now considering her options.

In contract law terms, what we saw for the first three months of the contract was full performance by both parties. In other words, they were both doing what they agreed to do. Had they continued to behave in this way, the contract would have run its course and ended after 12 months; the obligations of the parties would have been discharged by performance. However, in month four it appears that Ed breached his side of the bargain. He did deliver the produce to Davina but it was late. Note that the reasons why it was late are not generally relevant; he promised to deliver on the first working day of each month and he did not do that, therefore he breached the contract.

The first thing to note about a breach of contract is that it always gives the "innocent" party a right to claim damages (compensation) for any losses caused by the breach. Therefore Davina could, after the late delivery in the fourth month, have taken Ed to court and sued him for any losses she could show had arisen. For example, if she had run out of ingredients and could therefore not do any baking for a few days, she may well lose out on orders from her own customers. If so, she could sue for the lost profit from those orders. In reality, minor breaches of contracts occur very often. Assuming Davina carries a stock of ingredients and therefore had enough left over from the previous month, she probably wouldn't lose out and therefore is content to accept Ed's apology and leave it at that. Even if it caused her some inconvenience and a lost sale or two she may still choose not to take any further action. She could try to settle things without going to court, perhaps by asking for a reduction in the price for that month to reflect the fact that the delivery was late.

When it comes to the fifth month, Ed's delivery is three weeks late. This is clearly a much more serious breach of the same term of the contract than when he was a few days late. It may well be that Davina will want to bring the contract to an end now because she thinks that Ed will continue to deliver late and it will no doubt cause problems to her business.

Whether she can do this or not depends on what kind of term has been breached. In law there is an important distinction between contractual terms which are classed as "conditions" and contractual terms which are classed as "warranties". A condition is a term of the contract which goes to the heart of what the contract is about. In other words, it is a key contractual term involving an important aspect of the contract. A rather complex example is the case of *Bunge Corp v Tradax SA* (1981), in which the court said that the timing of a shipment was a condition in a shipping contract, as were other related terms. It was a central part of that contract that the ship left on time. A warranty is a term which is less important and not central to the main purpose of the contract.

The importance of the distinction between conditions and warranties is in the remedy which is available. We'll look more at remedies later, but basically the breach of a warranty allows the other party to sue for damages, whereas the breach of a condition allows the other party to terminate the contract.

If we think about Davina's business, then a condition of the contract is that Ed delivers certain ingredients to her each month. These are no doubt listed in the contract for certainty, and if he delivers the wrong ingredients, this will almost certainly be a breach of a condition and therefore Davina could terminate the contract then and there, freeing her to find an alternative supplier for the remainder of the contract.

If, on the other hand, there was a provision about the particular brand of chocolate to be included in the delivery, and Ed substituted this for a different brand, then this may well be deemed to be a breach of warranty and Davina could only sue for any loss she had suffered.

So what type of clause is the delivery clause? This could conceivably be a condition, especially if Davina has highlighted it as being particularly important for good reasons (such as the fact that she tended to run her stock right down to nothing each month to keep things fresh). It is probably unlikely to be a warranty because it is certainly of some importance, which brings us to the third and final classification of contractual terms, known as "innominate terms". This idea was developed in the case of *Hong Kong Fir Shipping Limited v Kawasaki Kisen Kaisha* (1962) and refers to a contractual term which is somewhere between a warranty and a condition. It is basically a term, the status of which really depends on the nature and effect of the actual breach that occurs. As we have seen in Davina's case, Ed could breach the delivery term by a very short period which may not have too much effect on her business. On the other hand he could breach it quite significantly (the fifth month delivery is now three weeks late) and this could have a serious impact on her business.

If the delivery clause is an innominate term, then the breach in the fourth month is probably only going to lead to a claim for compensation (in fact Davina overlooked the breach entirely) and the breach in the fifth month may well give rise to a right to terminate the contract. Davina could then find an alternative supplier for the remainder of the period if she wished to. It is worth noting that she does not *have* to terminate the contract, but if she does continue with it, then both parties remain bound to complete all their outstanding obligations.

We have seen in this chapter that a breach of a contractual term will give rise to a claim for compensation by the innocent party. If the term breached is an important term which goes to the heart of the contract (a condition) then the innocent party can also terminate the contract if they wish. Many contractual terms are not easily recognisable as conditions and warranties and it is only when an actual breach occurs that we can classify them as such. These terms are known as innominate terms. The parties may decide to label their terms as conditions, but the court can still look beyond this label to determine the importance of the clause and therefore whether it is a condition, a warranty or an innominate term.

Chapter 13 – Remedies

As discussed above, a party to a contract who suffers a breach is entitled as of right to monetary compensation by way of damages. Note that the purpose of contractual damages is to put the innocent party back into the position they would have been in had the contract been fulfilled as agreed. Damages are not about punishing the breaching party, and the fact that the breaching party may have themselves made a profit from the breach is not relevant when assessing the level of damages to be awarded by the court.

For example, take the situation involving Aaron and Beth from earlier in the book. They agreed that Beth would sell her car to Aaron and that he would pay £2,000 for it. If he went away to collect the money with which to buy the car and returned to find that Beth had, in the meantime, sold the car to someone else who offered her £2,200, then Beth would have breached her contract with Aaron. If Aaron sued Beth, he could only claim for his loss, not her profit. Beth has made a gain of £200 by breaching the contract and selling to someone else. This is not relevant to Aaron's loss. What has he actually lost from suffering this breach of contract? He could potentially claim any additional expenses he might incur in finding an alternative car. If he found an equivalent car elsewhere that cost more, he could potentially claim the difference between the £2,000 he agreed to pay to Beth and the price of the new car, but at that point it becomes difficult to prove that two cars are "equivalent" due to the potential differences (in age, mileage, condition and so on). Aaron might be angry that Beth breached the contract, and especially that she profited from doing so, but that is not relevant to assessing his losses.

On the other hand, a person who suffers a breach of contract can claim for the profit that they themselves have lost due to the breach. For example, if Davina, our baker from the last chapter loses bakery orders because she has run out of ingredients due to the late delivery by Ed, she can claim from Ed the losses that she suffers as a result.

Sometimes a person who has suffered a breach of contract may wish to recover expenses which have been incurred, and effectively lost due to the breach. This is generally allowed, as long as no "double" compensation occurs. This was seen in the case of *Anglia Television v Reed* (1972). When a key actor pulled out of the film and thereby breached his contract, the television company successfully claimed compensation based not on the profit it expected to make from the film (which would be speculative and therefore hard to determine) but on the expenditure they had incurred on producing the film up to that point.

Whether a person who has suffered a breach of contract sues for their lost profit, or for expenses incurred, they are focusing on the financial value of their perceived losses. However, contracts are often entered into for non-financial reasons and this can lead to problems when it comes to deciding the level of compensation payable for a breach of contract.

This was recognised in the case of *Ruxley Electronics and Construction Ltd v Forsyth* (1996). Mr Forsyth entered into a contract for the construction of a swimming pool in his garden. Once built, he noticed that it was in fact not as deep as he had requested in the contract. Although only too shallow by several inches, he asked the court for an amount of damages which would allow him to have the pool reconstructed to the correct depth. This is known as the "cost of cure" measure of damages. However, the court said this was disproportionate to the level of loss actually suffered and awarded him a significantly smaller sum of compensation.

Damages are calculated as the difference between the value of performance under the contract and the actual value of performance received. This "difference in value" basis was also considered in the *Ruxley* case above. The contractors who built the swimming pool produced evidence to the court that the value of the house with the "shallow" swimming pool was no different to the value of the house as it would have been with the pool built to the correct depth. As we saw above, the court found a "middle ground" solution and awarded compensation somewhere between the "difference in value" basis of nil and the full cost of putting the swimming pool right.

As a general rule the date of assessment of damages will be the date of the breach, or when the innocent party became aware of the breach if that is later.

Generally, the innocent party must prove that the breach of contract caused the losses which he or she is claiming. This is not usually a problem, but for example an act of the innocent party may be so unreasonable that it breaks that "chain of causation".

Another key point to consider is that of "remoteness of damage". Clearly a breach of contract could have a serious "knock on" effect; it could start a chain of events which result in huge losses being incurred. The case of *Hadley v Baxendale* (1854) is the leading case on remoteness of damage and helps us to determine when a particular loss might be too remote, or too far down the chain of events. In that case, it was decided that the innocent party could only claim for losses which occur naturally or as a result of the usual course of things after a breach of contract. It also held that the breaching party may be liable for losses that did not arise naturally but which were in the reasonable contemplation of both of the parties at the time the contract was entered into – in other words, known about and accepted by both.

The case of *Victoria Laundry (Windsor) Limited v Newman Industries Ltd* (1949) is a good example of how these conditions are applied. The laundry ordered a new boiler which was delivered late. Their claim for lost profits was allowed as "arising naturally" from the breach. However, the laundry also had a lucrative Government contract which resulted in much larger losses. The court decided that these losses were not recoverable because they did not "arise naturally" from the breach therefore if the laundry wanted to claim such losses the other party should have been informed about the Government contract before the contract for the boiler was entered into. This makes sense if you think about it, because the supplier of the boiler would know that if they deliver the boiler late, then they will be liable for any "normal" losses incurred. Had they known about the possibility of much larger losses, then they might have increased the price they quote for the boiler to cover the risk, or simply taken more care to ensure that the boiler was delivered on time.

Another important principle relating to damages is that a person who suffers a breach of contract is generally under a duty to take all reasonable steps to mitigate their loss. In other words, they are under a duty to reduce their loss as far as reasonably possible. For example, if a builder finds that one of his customers has cancelled the contract he had with them to build an extension, the builder cannot simply sit back and sue for the profit that they would have made had the contract been performed as agreed. The builder is under an obligation to go out and try to find replacement work. If this new work is at least as profitable as the cancelled work, then no loss has arisen from the breach of contract. The rationale for this is that it is good for the general efficiency of the economy that people should be "busy", even though the rule may at first seem a little unfair on the innocent party.

Another important issue here is the availability of damages for losses which go beyond financial loss. The starting point is that the law of contract does not compensate for disappointment, hurt feelings or distress caused by the mere fact of a contract being breached. In the case of *Addis v Gramophone Co Limited* (1909) the court refused to take into account mental distress when a manager was wrongfully sacked for alleged dishonesty. There are however some exceptions to this general rule. For example, where the main object of the contract is to obtain some mental satisfaction, damages for disappointment may be awarded to compensate for the loss of that expected benefit. A good example of this is a contract for a holiday such as the case of *Jarvis v Swan Tours* (1973).

In the case of *Farley v Skinner* (2001), a surveyor was asked to report on a house including whether noise could be a problem due to its proximity to Gatwick airport. The surveyor said noise was unlikely to be a problem and was found to be in breach of contract. The court decided that it is enough if the term breached was one which both parties knew to be important – the contract as a whole did not need to be for some mental satisfaction. This was satisfied on the facts as the defendant had specifically asked the surveyor to report on noise.

Before we move on to look briefly at other remedies which are available on a breach of contract, one final point to consider is that sometimes the parties to a contract may wish to try to predetermine the level of compensation payable on breach. This is referred to as a liquidated damages clause. The clause must be one which genuinely attempts to quantify the loss that will result on breach. If it does that, then it will be a valid contractual clause. The amount of liquidated damages will be paid regardless of whether the loss is more or less than the amount agreed. This should be contrasted to a penalty clause, which is a clause which tries to ensure a breach does not occur by setting the level of "compensation" at an extravagant level. These clauses are not enforceable. The rules for determining if a clause is a penalty clause or a liquidated damages clause were set out by the court in *Dunlop Pneumatic Tyre Co v New Garage and Motor Co Ltd* (1915).

      Finally for this chapter we need to consider briefly a couple of other remedies which are available in certain situations on a breach of contract. Imagine that you entered into a contract to buy an original painting. The person who agreed to sell you the painting then changes their mind and returns any money you have paid. You may feel in this case that a claim for compensation is not helpful to you. That is because the painting was an original and therefore by definition only one of its kind exists. Damages to cover your expenses of finding an alternative is simply not what you want. In cases such as this you can ask the court for the remedy of specific performance. This remedy is only available where you can prove to the court that damages are not adequate. If the court agrees, then the person with whom you contracted is ordered to perform the contract as originally agreed. In other words, they would have to hand over the painting to you (and you would, of course, have to pay for it). It is particularly useful where the subject matter of the contract is unique in some way. A good example is land, because every plot of land is unique. There are situations where the court will not make such an order, even if you can show that damages are not really adequate. For example, if the subject matter (the painting in our example) has been sold to someone else in the meantime.

The final remedy I want to mention is that of injunction. You may well have heard of these before. It is an order made by the court that a person should refrain from doing something they promised not to do or should take positive steps to rectify something they have done which they promised not to do. An example would be where someone builds on land where they have promised not to in a contract. Again, it will be essential to persuade the court that an award of damages will not be adequate compensation.

We have covered quite a lot in this chapter, but the key point is that the main remedy for breach of contract is an award of compensation to the "innocent" party. The level of compensation, or damages, is set by reference to the loss suffered by the innocent party. That loss must not be too remote or too far away from the breach of contract, and it can include expenses incurred in reliance on the fact that the contract will be performed. We have also seen the courts facing a dilemma when the cost of putting things right is huge compared to the actual breach, or where the breach has in fact caused no loss of value to the subject matter of the contract. In those cases the court must somehow value the lost ability to use the subject matter to quite the same extent as was envisaged in the contract. We have also considered damages for distress and loss of enjoyment and seen how the courts have been more willing to allow such claims in recent times. Finally, we have looked at the alternative remedies of specific performance and injunction.

Chapter 14 – Misrepresentation

Earlier in the book when we looked at the terms of a contract, we saw that statements made in the course of negotiations could become terms of the contract or they could be deemed to be representations. Terms, we decided, were statements that were clearly of importance to the recipient, or were made near to the time of formation of the contract, or were made by someone who has expert knowledge of the situation. We have since seen that when a term of the contract is breached, that breach of contract leads to certain remedies being available to the party suffering the breach (usually an award of compensation, called damages).

We said at that time that we would return to representations later in the book. Remember they are statements made which do not form part of the contract, but which have nonetheless induced the other party to enter into the contract. If a representation turns out to be false, then it potentially becomes a misrepresentation, and the effect of that is what this chapter is about. This is a reasonably complex area and so this chapter will only look at the basic position.

Misrepresentations can be made in writing or orally. The courts have also decided that certain types of conduct can amount to a misrepresentation. In the case of *Gordon v Sellico* (1986) the seller of a property deliberately covered up the dry rot in the property and the court said that by doing so they had misrepresented that the property did not suffer from dry rot.

A misrepresentation must be significant and not trivial. It should also be a statement of fact and generally not an opinion or a statement of future intention. It must also be known to the recipient and the maker must intend that the statement is relied upon, and it must actually be relied upon by the recipient. These aspects can lead to difficulties and all have relevant case law to help understand their application, but in a book of this nature we cannot cover all the details here. Basically, a statement of fact which turns out to be false, which the recipient relied on to make their decision on the contract, may well turn out to be a misrepresentation.

If we think back to Aaron and his search for a car, we talked about the possibility of him visiting a car dealer, "Carl's Cars". When the dealer, Carl, was talking to Aaron about the possible sale of the car, he may well have made various statements about the car. Some of those statements will undoubtedly become terms of the contract. One obvious example is the price; this will no doubt be included in the written contract that they both sign.

The contract may also have a brief description of the car so that Aaron is comfortable that on signing the contract he is buying the right car. However, the contract may well not have details of the age, condition and mileage of the car for example. If Carl has made statements about these things to Aaron, then he is making statements of fact, which are presumably intended to induce or persuade Aaron to enter into the contract. They may not be contractual terms but they are likely to be at least representations. If any turn out to be false, then they will be misrepresentations.

It is important to note that there are three types of misrepresentation which in turn affect the remedies available to the innocent party. The first type is a fraudulent misrepresentation. This is where the person who makes the statement lacks the honest belief that the statement is true. It is often difficult to prove that someone has acted dishonestly, but if that hurdle can be overcome, the remedy available is generous. Basically, all direct losses, including consequential losses, resulting from the misrepresentation can be recovered. This is clearly more wide-reaching than the usual rule for compensation in contract law. For example, the limits imposed in the case of *Hadley v Baxendale* (1854), regarding remoteness do not apply here.

The second type of misrepresentation is called negligent misrepresentation. This can then be sub-divided into two categories. The first category of negligent misrepresentation has been constructed through the decisions of the courts over the years, as we have seen for much of the rest of the law of contract. This category is referred to as negligent misstatement. This is where someone makes a statement and in doing so assumes a duty of care to make sure that the statement is accurate. There usually needs to be a close relationship between the two parties, although not a contractual relationship as such. A well-known case here is that of *Caparo Industries plc v Dickman* (1990). In that case accountants who had checked the accounts of a company were not liable to someone who then relied on those accounts for their own purposes. The accounts had been checked on behalf of the company to which they related, and not with a view to them being used and relied upon by other people. Therefore the accountants did not have to pay damages to the other person when it turned out that the accounts were misleading. If they had, then damages are paid on the same basis as a claim for negligence generally, which is outside the scope of this book, but based on whether the losses would be a reasonably foreseeable consequence of the misrepresentation, albeit remote.

The second category of negligent misrepresentation is contained in the

Misrepresentation Act 1967. We have mentioned before that much of contract law is made up of the decisions of the court. In this case there is a short piece of legislation (an Act of Parliament) which covers the position. Under this Act, a person who makes a false statement which induces another person to enter into a contract with them, is liable for negligent misrepresentation unless they can show that they had reasonable grounds for believing that the statement was true. Unlike negligent misstatement which we looked at above, this does not require a special relationship to exist, but it only applies where a contractual relationship arises. The level of damages which can be claimed for this type of negligent misrepresentation was set in the case of *Royscot Trust Limited v Rogerson* (1991) in which the court decided that all losses could be recovered regardless of whether they were foreseeable.

The third and final type of misrepresentation is called "innocent misrepresentation". As the name suggests, this is where someone makes a representation for which they have reasonable grounds for believing is true, but which nonetheless turns out to be false. This type of misrepresentation does not give a right to damages, only a right to rescind the contract, which is a concept we will look at now.

All types of misrepresentation (fraudulent, negligent or innocent) give rise to the right to rescind the contract. This means that the person who has suffered the misrepresentation can cancel or "void" the contract, which has the effect of putting the parties back into the position they would have been in had the contract never been entered into. The right to rescind the contract can be lost, for example if it becomes impossible to put the parties back into their pre-contractual positions or if the person exercising the right to rescind takes too long to do so. A final point worth remembering about the right to rescind is that the court has discretion under the Misrepresentation Act 1967 to make an award of damages instead of allowing the contract to be rescinded if it thinks that is a fairer way of dealing with things. This will prevent contracts being brought to an end due to trivial misrepresentations.

In this chapter we have defined a misrepresentation as a false statement of fact which induces another person to enter into a contract. We have seen that three types of misrepresentation exist and what level of damages is payable in respect of each. We have also considered the alternative remedy of rescinding the contract.

Chapter 15 – Exclusion clauses

This is the final substantive area of law that I want to look at in this book. As with some of the other topics, this is a complex issue which could quite easily form the subject of a separate book! However, the purpose of this book is to give you a basic introduction to the topic so let's do that now.

We have looked at how contracts are formed and what happens when they are broken. The usual remedy for the innocent party is an award of compensation based on the loss incurred by the breach of contract. An exclusion clause is a clause which tries to exclude or limit liability in some way; in other words, a clause which tries to "get me off the hook" when I breach my contract.

There are three questions which need to be answered when looking at the validity of an exclusion clause. Firstly, has the clause been incorporated into the contract? In other words, has it been introduced at the right time and in the right way to become a term of the contract? Secondly, does the clause cover the type of liability which caused the losses? More on this later. Thirdly, are there any pieces of legislation (statutes, or Acts of Parliament) which may work to invalidate the clause? Let's take each of these points in turn.

We touched on whether a term is incorporated into a contract when we looked at contractual terms earlier in the book. We said then that the question most commonly arises in relation to exclusion clauses. Let's remind ourselves of what we said back then.

We said that the most obvious way to incorporate a term into a contract is for the contract to be written out and signed by both parties. In the case of L'*Estrange v Graucob* (1934) it was decided that if someone signs a written contract, then as long as no fraud has taken place, they are bound by the terms of the contract even if they have not read it.

We also saw that a key thing to remember is that terms can only be incorporated if they are added *before* the contract is formed. A good example is the case of *Olley v Marlborough Court Limited* (1949) in which the contract for the hire of a hotel room was completed at reception, so that any further statements made in the room itself could not form part of the contract. In that case a notice on the back of the hotel room door attempting to exclude liability on the part of the hotel was held not to be incorporated into the contract and therefore of no legal effect.

Another point to keep in mind is that if the term is written down, it must be included within a document that a person would reasonably expect to contain contractual terms. For example, in the case of *Chapelton v Barry UDC* (1940) the court decided that a receipt for the hire of a deck chair was not such a document. In addition, clauses which are particularly onerous, and this will include many exclusion clauses, should be highlighted in some way or specifically brought to the attention of the other contracting party. This can be seen in operation in the case of *Interfoto Picture v Stiletto Visual Programmes (*1989).

Finally here, it is worth mentioning that terms can be incorporated into a contract based on the previous dealings between the parties. In other words, if they have dealt with each other before many times then the court may decide that the terms on which they have previously contracted also apply to the current contract.

Once we are satisfied that the exclusion clause has been incorporated into the contract and can therefore potentially be relied upon, the second thing we need to consider is whether it covers the type of liability which caused the losses. This is where things get very complex, but we'll keep it as simple as we can. In fact, whilst the interpretation of the clause used to be an important "weapon" for the courts in countering an exclusion clause which they viewed as being unfair, due to the legislation which now covers this topic such wordplay has become less important. What the court is doing here is assessing the wording used by the parties in the exclusion clause and deciding whether it actually works to exclude the liability that has actually arisen. If there is any ambiguity, then the court will use this against the person who is trying to rely on the exclusion clause. As I said above, things get rather complicated here, but one example is that the courts take the view that it is unlikely that a party to a contract would want to allow the other party to exclude liability for their own negligence. Negligence is basically carelessness and can arise between two people even where there is no contractual relationship. If I contract with someone on the basis that they will provide a service to me, I would not expect them to be able to perform that service in a careless manner and then find that I had no remedy in law against them. The court has therefore developed a rule that states that to exclude negligence, very clear language to that effect must be used in the contract, with specific reference to the term "negligence" or a similar term. This can be seen in operation in the case of *White v John Warwick Co Limited* (1953). When someone hired a cycle which caused them injury, the exclusion clause did not specifically refer to negligence. The court decided that whilst the clause had successfully excluded liability for the breach of contract (effectively hiring out a cycle which was not safe), it did not work to exclude a general claim for negligence.

Finally for this chapter, we need to look at the relevant legislation. This starts to encroach into another area of law known as "consumer law", which is a collection of laws which operate to protect consumers (customers) when they deal with businesses. Other legislation applies to contracts between two businesses, known as the Unfair Contract Terms Act 1977. For the moment we will stick to the position relating to consumers, which we find in the Consumer Rights Act 2015.

Generally, the Consumer Rights Act applies to contractual relationships where at least one party is acting in the course of a business - in other words, not to private agreements between two individuals. It would not generally apply therefore to the sale by Beth of her car to Aaron that we looked at earlier in the book. It would however apply to the sale of a car by Carl the car dealer to Aaron that we also considered.

One of the first things that the Act does is to make it clear that liability for negligence which causes death or personal injury to a person cannot be excluded by a contractual term or a notice. That means that the injury caused by the faulty cycle in the *White* case above could not be excluded now because the Act would make such a term invalid.

The Act does allow negligence liability to be excluded in relation to other types of damage, but mere knowledge of such a term does not mean that the consumer has therefore accepted the risk. For example, if the rider in the *White* case damaged their watch when falling from the cycle, the hiring company could exclude negligence liability for that damage if they could convince the court it was fair to do so.

Returning to the position of two businesses contracting with each other, the Unfair Contract Terms Act 1977 also restricts the exclusion of negligence liability, as well as covering breaches of contract where a business deals on the standard terms of another business. The problem with standard terms is that they are generally not open for negotiation and are often presented on a "take it or leave it" basis. In these situations liability for breach of contract can only be excluded where it is reasonable to do so.

When we looked at the terms of a contract in Chapter 8, we also looked briefly at the Sale of Goods Act 1979 and the Consumer Rights Act 2015, and noted that these Acts imply certain terms into contracts to protect contracting parties. The final thing to note about the Unfair Contract Terms Act 1977 and the Consumer Rights Act 2015, is that they restrict the extent to which liability for breaching these implied terms can be excluded. Generally this cannot be done when dealing with a consumer and must be reasonable when dealing with another business.

So to recap for this chapter, we have seen that liability for breach of contract can potentially be excluded by using a contractual term. That term must be incorporated into the contract, and it may have to be highlighted to the other party. It also needs to be clearly worded, especially if it is attempting to exclude liability for negligence. We have seen that negligence liability cannot be excluded in any event if it results in death or personal injury due to legislation, which also restricts the use of exclusion clauses in other situations.

List of Cases

Links are to the *main* reference in the text.

Adams v Lindsell (1818) – if an acceptance is posted, then as long as certain conditions are met, it can be effective at the time of posting rather than when it is received by the offeror

Addis v Gramophone Co Limited (1909) – damages are not generally available to compensate for disappointment or hurt feelings

Anglia Television v Reed (1972) – damages can be claimed for expenses incurred in reliance on the contract being performed as agreed

Balfour v Balfour (1919) – the parties to social and domestic agreements are presumed to lack the intention to create legally binding contracts

Bannerman v White (1861) – if a statement made by one party is particularly important to the other party, then it is likely to form a term of the contract between them

Blackpool and Fylde Aero Club Limited v Blackpool Borough Council (1990) – a request for tenders can lead to an obligation to actually consider (but not necessarily accept) all tenders received which are in accordance with the tender request

British Crane Hire Corporation Limited v Ipswich Plant Hire Limited (1975) – the court can imply terms into a contract based on trade custom and practice

Bunge Corp v Tradax SA (1981) – an example of a condition, which is a contractual term going to the heart of the contract

Butler Machine Tool Co. Limited v Ex-Cell-O Corporation (England) Limited (1979) – in a "battle of forms" situation, the court tries to determine which set of terms and conditions were finally accepted and therefore included in the contract

Carlill v Carbolic Smoke Ball Co. (1893) – example of an advertisement which was deemed to be a unilateral contract

Caparo Industries plc v Dickman (1990) – there generally needs to be a close relationship between the parties for negligent misstatement to apply

Chapelton v Barry UDC (1940) – a written contractual term must be included within a document that a person would reasonably expect to contain contractual terms

Chappell & Co. Ltd v Nestle Co. Ltd (1960) – consideration needs to be something of value in the eyes of the law, but need not be commercially sufficient

Couturier v Hastie (1856) – a contract for the sale of goods which had already been sold was void due to mistake

Currie v Misa (1875) – definition of consideration as benefit received or detriment suffered

Davis Contractors Limited v Fareham UDC (1956) – a contract will not be frustrated simply because contractual obligations have become more difficult to perform

Dick Bentley Productions Limited v Harold Smith (Motors) Limited (1965) – a statement made by an expert is likely to constitute a term of the contract

Dickinson v Dodds (1876) – revocation of an offer can be communicated to the offeree from any reliable source, not just the offeror

Dunlop Pneumatic Tyre Co Limited v New Garage and Motor Co Ltd (1915) – if a liquidated damages clause sets the level of "agreed"

damages too high, the clause will potentially not be valid due to it being a penalty clause

Dunlop Pneumatic Tyre Co Limited v Selfridge & Co Limited (1915) – defines consideration as being given in return for the promise made by the other party

Errington v Errington and Woods (1952) – a unilateral contract cannot be revoked once performance of the requested act has been started

Esso Petroleum Co. Ltd v Commissioners of Customs and Excise (1976) – there is a presumption that the parties to a commercial contract do intend to be legally bound by that contract

Farley v Skinner (2001) – damages may exceptionally be claimed for mental distress where both parties are aware that that is an important element of the contract

Felthouse v Bindley (1862) – silence by the recipient of an offer cannot generally be deemed to signify that the recipient has accepted the offer

Gordon v Sellico (1986) – a person's conduct can amount to a misrepresentation

Hadley v Baxendale (1854) – a party who suffers a breach of contract can only claim losses which arise naturally from the breach or which are reasonably contemplated by both parties when the contract was made

Holwell Securities Limited v Hughes (1974) – acceptance is effective when it has been communicated to the person making the offer

Hong Kong Fir Shipping Limited v Kawasaki Kisen Kaisha (1962) – an innominate term is a contractual term whose classification as a condition or a warranty is impossible without knowing the effect of the actual breach which occurs

Hyde v Wrench (1840) – example of a counter-offer, which has the effect of rejecting the original offer and replacing it with a new one

Interfoto Picture v Stiletto Visual Programmes (1989) – a particularly onerous contractual term should be specifically highlighted to the other contracting party

Investors Compensation Scheme Limited v West Bromwich Building Society (1998) - the court will try its best to interpret contract clauses as a reasonable person would understand them to read, having regard to anything available to the parties which might influence this understanding.

<u>Jarvis v Swan Tours (1973)</u> – contracts which are specifically for enjoyment or relaxation, such as holiday bookings, may give rise to a claim for compensation for lost enjoyment if they are breached

<u>Krell v Henry (1903)</u> – a contract can be frustrated when the main purpose (as envisaged by both parties) of the contract is no longer attainable

<u>L'*Estrange v Graucob* (1934)</u> – if someone signs a written contract, then as long as no fraud has taken place, they are bound by the terms of the contract even if they have not read it

<u>Leaf v International Galleries (1950)</u> – a mistake as to the quality of the item being sold will not generally be enough for the courts to void the contract because the contract can still be performed as agreed

<u>Lewis v Avery (1972)</u> – mistaken identity in a face to face situation often results in the court assuming that the seller intended to deal with the actual physical person in front of them, whoever that may actually be

<u>Liverpool City Council v Irwin (1977)</u> – a term can be implied into a contract by the courts on the basis that the term is a necessary feature of that type of contract

<u>Merritt v Merritt</u> (1970) – legally binding agreements can arise between spouses after the marriage has broken down

<u>Moorcock (The)</u> (1889) – the court will generally only imply terms into a particular contract where it is necessary to reflect the apparent intentions of the parties and to make the contract work

<u>Olley v Marlborough Court Limited (1949)</u> – statements made after a contract is entered into cannot form part of the contract as they have been made too late

<u>Oscar Chess Limited v Williams (1957)</u> – a statement made by a "non-expert" is likely to be a representation rather than a term of the contract

<u>Partridge v Crittenden (1968)</u> – advertisements are generally classed as invitations to treat rather than as offers for sale

<u>Payne v Cave (1789)</u> – offers can be revoked before acceptance. Also, <u>a request for</u>

bids by the auctioneer at an auction is an invitation to treat not an offer for sale

Pharmaceutical Society of Great Britain v Boots Cash Chemists (Southern) Limited (1952) – a display of goods in a shop is generally an invitation to treat and not an offer for sale

Ramsgate Victoria Hotel Co v Montefiore (1866) – an offer will lapse after a reasonable time has passed since it was made

Roscorla v Thomas (1842) – past consideration is not valid consideration as it has already been provided and therefore not valid for the present agreement

Routledge v Grant (1828) – offers can be revoked even where the offeror agrees to keep the offer open for a period of time

Routledge v McKay (1954) – statements made some time before the contract is entered into are likely to be classed as representations and not terms of the contract

Royscot Trust Limited v Rogerson (1991) – following a negligent misrepresentation, all losses can be recovered regardless of whether they are foreseeable

Ruxley Electronics and Construction Ltd v Forsyth (1996) – the court will not award damages to "put things right" if that is disproportionate to the consequences caused by the breach

Scammell and Nephew Limited v Ouston (1941) – if the terms of a contract are unclear, the court may well decide that the contract is unenforceable

Shogan Finance Limited v Norman Hudson (2002) – mistaken identity in a written contract often results in the court assuming that the seller intended to deal with the person actually named in the contract

Smith v Hughes (1871) – when a mistake is made in the formation of a contract, the court will often look to see which party's interpretation of the situation is most reasonable

Spencer v Harding (1870) – a request for tenders is generally an invitation to treat and not an offer for sale

Stilk v Myrick (1809) – the performance of an existing contractual duty owed to someone cannot generally be valid consideration for a further promise from the same person

Taylor v Caldwell (1863) – an agreement for the hire of a concert hall was frustrated when the concert hall burnt down

Victoria Laundry (Windsor) Limited v Newman Industries Ltd (1949) – if "higher than normal" losses are likely to arise following a breach of contract, then this should be advised to the other contracting party to avoid such losses being too remote

White v John Warwick Co Limited (1953) – to exclude liability for negligence, the contract term must be very clear and specifically refer to "negligence" or an equivalent word

List of Statutes

Links are to the *main* reference in the text.

Consumer Rights Act 2015

Law Reform (Frustrated Contracts) Act 1943

Misrepresentation Act 1967

Sale of Goods Act 1979

Unfair Contract Terms Act 1977

Printed in Great Britain
by Amazon